T0369184

Adrift

KELLE KEYLES

authorHOUSE®

AuthorHouse™
1663 Liberty Drive
Bloomington, IN 47403
www.authorhouse.com
Phone: 1-800-839-8640

First published by AuthorHouse 5/12/2011

ISBN: 978-1-4567-5362-7 (e)
ISBN: 978-1-4567-5363-4 (sc)

Library of Congress Control Number: 2011907748

Printed in the United States of America

This book is dedicated to Amna Chowdhrey
and Zahra Jasdanwala, who inspired this book
and to Tai Walker, who helped me through it all.

Ticking Clocks

Time wastes away by itself,
There is no reason to speed up this process,
Time is more valuable than money,
But all the money in the world can't buy more time,
Or can it,
Money buys doctors who can help you stay on this earth
up to the last minute you can stand,
What good is being alive if everyone you love isn't?

Emotional Shipwreck

When you lose your mind,
you will know it,
Your life will begin to fall apart one by one,
You will start to put it back together,
But it will just fall apart twice as fast,
No aspect of your life will feel safe,
You will be an undocked boat on the rough seas of life,
Until you find that one person,
Your dock,
Your day will begin and end with them,
You will owe them everything,
Nothing else will compare to your need to pay them back that debt.

Forgiveness

Now this is more than a word,
It is worth more than all the gold in the world,
But sadly you can't buy forgiveness,
Forgiveness is a feeling, an action, a gift that only can be given.

Sorry

Sorry is over used,
Sorry is a word that doesn't mean much without a why,
Sorry is a word that needs a definition behind it,
Sorry is the type of word with our without a definition
You can't be sure it works.

Sadness

Sadness is in everyone,
Is the reason **why** making you sad,
Why doesn't someone confront you when they are mad?
Why do we think giving up is ok?
I am not sure, but I'm determined to find out.

Gone

Gone far away,
Never came back not today,
You said it would be a while,
I miss you and your smile,
I count the days that go by,
Can't wait till you say hi,
Mad as mad could be,
I hope you will forgive me!

For Amna c.

Closure

Everyone needs a taste of closure,
To help them move on to happier times,
Without closure,
you will always have a sore spot in your heart.

Self Lies

How can you hate if you never knew,
How can you hate if you never envied,
How can you hate if you never were jealous,
How can you so intensely hate if you never loved?

Ripple

Such an intense relationship,
Closer than you are with family,
Blind trust,
On the outside it looks like a brick wall,
But in reality it is a thin sheet of glass,
Even the tiniest move will shatter it,
Beyond repair,
Maybe you were better off as just friends,
A deep connection that crushes the soul,
Forever changing how both of you see the world.

Surrounded by all but them

No matter the amount of friends you acquire,
How much they all love you,
You will still seek the connection,
With the one who isn't hypnotized by you,
Forget about them you tell yourself,
But in turn they are all you think about.

Time hurts

You hurt so badly,
But you must stay strong,
All your friends need you,
Depend on you to solve their problems,
When you were friends it was like bliss,
But was it?
You alter memories,
Was it really that amazingly filled with trust and joy,
You don't care,
You tell yourself you will never move on,
But you will,
Time only makes it harder.

Reflections

Apologizing doesn't erase what you did,
It is burned into memories,
You can't change how they feel,
You can't take it back,
It haunts you,
You go over how you should have changed it,
But it is a waste of time to live in the past,
Because you can never change it,
You can only change, create the future.

Bleak

Life is empty,
In reality it is full,
Filled with people,
Pasts, presents, futures, emotions, personalities,
People love each and everyone,
They are all special,
Life doesn't have a price,
Life is sacred and so easily taken for granted,
Every individual is different in their own way.

Fury

Each day may be your last,
Why waste it on hate,
Anger will eat away at you,
You will push away the ones who love you,
Misplaced anger is so dangerous,
Deadly,
Friendships will be lost,
Anger will consume you if you let it.

Barbells

A dark depression will arise,
Pull you down,
Into the deep dark depths of the unknown,
You think it holds you back,
But it teaches you,
To act different next time,
It enlightens you,
It opens your sealed eyes to the harshness of the world.
For Anna Z

Breath

A depression you can't get out from under,
Its weight increases,
Oblivious to the world around you,
Living in a haze,
Struggling to wear a smile,
You just want to crawl up into a ball,
Alone forever,
Nothing is important,
Your appetite doesn't grab your attention,
Let someone hold the weight for you,
Just for a while,
Until you can deal with it.

Statistics

You build up your confidence,
You know exactly what to say,
You walk into the room,
As soon as you see them your mind gets whipped clean,
You can't find the words,
You struggle to speak,
Everything isn't black and white,
It looks different on paper than in reality,
But it's better this way,
You own your life,
And you know what you want,
You also know what is good for you,
But sometimes you just don't care.

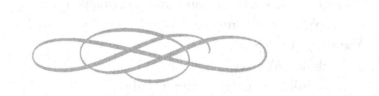

Door Mat

They own you,
Until you stop them,
Step up to the plate,
Take your life into your own hands,
If you don't you will be just like them,
Even though you hate them,
You need to fight,
Be a lover not a fighter,
But fight for what you love,
Stand up for yourself,
If you don't, who will?

Regret

The real reason you want someone back so much when you lose them is
because you know how much you hurt them and hate yourself for it,
If only you could have a re-do,
Start over,
You would treat them like royalty,
How they deserve to be treated,
You hate yourself for treating them bad,
And don't even know who that person was that hurt them,
You just know they look like you,
Sound like you,
But that was you then
This is you now.

Invisible baggage

You try to get over all the things that have hurt you,
But even the smallest ones are cemented in your head,
You try to run away from your problems,
But you are reminded of them every day,
Everyone has an invisible history,
You can't see it,
And they wish they couldn't either,
But sometimes you have a special memory
And you feel it slipping away,
You try to hold onto it,
But it runs right through your hands,
Our minds can be oh so cruel,
But every once in a while they will let you revisit your memory in a
Dream,
But when you wake up again your feeling of emptiness is amplified,
And the pain rushes back in,
Leaving you wishing you never had that dream again.

What's there, is there

Feelings that you can't control,
They consume you,
You can show them,
Or you don't,
Either way,
They are there,
You can't control them,
Even if you suppress them,
They will eventually rise to the surface,
Bottling them up will hurt you,
Express yourself,
No one can hold that against you.

Timeless bonds

They hurt you bad,
Betrayed,
But you can't ignore them,
The trust was glitched,
But you want to restore it,
You don't want to lose them,
And they don't want to lose you,
But now there is a distance,
Every time you see them you feel the pain,
If only for a split second,
But it is still there.

Trust yourself

Time and time again you will be hurt,
It will make you stronger,
After it makes you weak first,
You will be more cautions next time,
But that caution could kill you,
Thinking twice isn't always best.

Dangling Redemption

Forgiveness is power,
A taunting power,
People will bow down to you for it,
You could tease them with it and cause them pain,
The feeling of messing up a friendship is like no other,
The guilt,
The shame,
The heavy heart wears you down,
Forgiveness should be given or revoked,
Don't play with it,
Make a decision,
And stick to it.

Other side of the pillow

Friends come and go,
But guilt builds every minute,
Sorrow builds,
The doubt makes your heart heavy,
You won't be rid of it,
Why torture yourself if you can't change it,
Don't play it back in your head over and over,
Let your conscious rest tonight,
For tomorrow is a new day,
And tomorrow you can be a new person.

Rage really does blind us

Why fight violence with more violence,
Why add on to an already bad situation,
Why fight hate with hate,
When you can easily fight with love,
Why fight fire with fire,
When you can easily fight with water,
Fighting fire with fire only makes a bigger flame that will burn
everyone.

Time

Some people say time will live forever,
That it is continuous,
That time never stops,
That when humans are extinct, time will live on,
But is there really time when there's no one to count it,
If a tree falls and no one is around to hear it, does it still make a
sound,
How would anyone know if they weren't around to hear it.

Change is important

People continuously change,
On the inside and out,
You would not notice it,
But it happens,
We change into better versions of ourselves,
Some people can't accept that,
But it is true,
With every day we live we get wiser,
We change,
But not always for the better.

Pen and Paper

A place you control,
You create,
All actions come from your pencil,
A dictator of words.

Everlasting pit

You seem so far away,
But truly you are close,
A tiny step needs to be taken,
So much time has passed,
It hurts too much,
When we think of each other our souls fall,
Deeply saddened,
Forever we shall be.

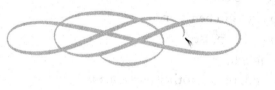

Pain You Can't Bare

Every day is a struggle,
Getting through the day without a meltdown is so hard,
Being distant,
So no one can look inside and see the pain,
Can't let people in for the fear of discovery,
Can't get five minutes of their time,
They hurt so bad,
But no one's there,
So alone in this world,
People are close but not close enough,
Only a few know their true life,
The pain and loneliness,
When they are sad they want to be able to hug their mom
But they can't... she isn't really there.
Sometimes they wish someone will help them,
They need it so much,
But no one looks close enough,
To see the lost child,
Looking for family....parents...love.

Tortured Soul

Inspired by Anna Z, a great friendship cut short.

It is so hard to believe you can be best friends one day and
enemies the next,
Good memories are best dwelled upon,
But that turning point plays like a broken record,
Trying to change the outcome,
Your dreams will reunite you with them,
When you awake your heart will feel empty,
I have learned it is best not to sleep,
That split second when you realize they are out of your reach is the
worst in the world,
Once you have felt this pain you will gladly welcome hell to your door.